DAUGHTER OF COURAGE

A CRY FOR JUSTICE

BY

BARBARA ANN MARY MACK

ISBN: 1-4033-7283-7 (e-book)
ISBN: 1-4033-7284-5 (Paperback)

This book is printed on acid free paper.

1stBooks – rev. 01/30/03

DEDICATION

This book is dedicated to all of the courageous daughters, who carried out God's mission, in spite of obstacles.

TABLE OF CONTENTS

ACKNOWLEDGMENT

I would like to offer my deepest gratitude to Almighty God, because He has inspired me to compose another book of inspiration in three days.

I thank Him for choosing me to convey His powerful messages of love to all.

"I thank You O Lord."

INTRODUCTION

Although being a servant of the Lord, requires humility and patience, he or she must also, express the gift of courage; especially when justice is concerned.

Being courageous also includes the acknowledgment of compassion and mercy, when dealing with issues concerning the well being of God's people.

One must exercise, the acts of compassion and mercy in obscure situations. A servant of the Lord, doesn't falter, or deviate from his or her assignment. because of fear or threats.

With the promise of hope, the servant of the Lord, continues to trust in Him at all times, because only God's words of comfort will help His servants, complete their tasks.

A servant of the Lord, must express the gift of obedience at all times, if he or she desires to please the Father of Love.

Daughter of Courage, expresses a continuous dialogue between God and His Spiritual Daughter, and their spiritual union. A Union that express unconditional love.

CHAPTER ONE: DAUGHTER OF COURAGE

Woman of courage, go out and proclaim My good news.

Share My words of everlasting life, with your family who sits in

My pews.

Tell them of My perfect ways that they must follow.

Tell them, My daughter, that if they want to see My glory, their

pride they must swallow.

Pride is an evil that they must part,

so that I can enter a clean and pure heart.

DAUGHTER OF COURAGE

Daughter of courage, walk with Me through your streets of sin and pain.

So that I can save your brothers and sisters, and your mission will not be in vain

Do not weep, My daughter, because I know how you feel.

I will save your brothers and sisters, because it is in My will.

Give thanks to your Lord, who loves all of His babes,

because He is the eternal Father, who always save.

DAUGHTER OF COURAGE

O daughter of courage, do not falter or stumble from the fear that comes with their taunting voices.

Do not back away with fear, because I am with you as you approach their unkind and tormenting words.

Take My hand as you approach My throne of consolation, My daughter.

I will lead you to My altar of peace, as they slash out at you with their words of hate.

My daughter, do not cringe when you hear their mumbles of mockery,

because I will drive away your foes, with the force of My love.

DAUGHTER OF COURAGE

Woman of courage, can you come closer to Me? So that I can share

with you the plans that I have for thee.

I will shower you with My everlasting love, so that you will have

the peace that comes from above.

My love will conquer all of the evils around you.

while you deliver My messages of courage to the faithful few.

O daughter of courage remain faithful and strong.

And My love will protect you, all day long.

I have blessed you with the gift of courage and might.

So that you can proclaim My messages throughout the night.

DAUGHTER OF COURAGE

Daughter of courage, can you hear your Father's call?

He is calling you into a holy and pure life.

A life that requires love and courage, My daughter.

Can you hear Me whispering My words of wisdom to you?

Can you grasp the meaning of My eternal words?

Listen closely, as I reveal My self to you, O daughter of great

courage.

Will you run with My words like a child with a new toy?

Will you share them with My searching children?

O daughter of courage, will you hold on to My words?

DAUGHTER OF COURAGE

My daughter, your courage is an everlasting gift that I have

bestowed upon you.

Express the gift of courage in your daily life, so that all may see

our divine union.

Pick up your shield, and follow Me. My words, O daughter, is your

armor, when you are on the battle field.

My words, are your strength, when weakness arises in you.

My words, are the hope that will get you through.

My words, are the weapon that will protect you from the evil one's

lies.

My words, O daughter of courage, are the joy, that never dies.

DAUGHTER OF COURAGE

Daughter of courage, will you stand up for justice, when My little ones welfare is in jeopardy?

Will you stand up for them, when they lose faith in Me?

Will you stand up for them, when they curse and swear at you?

Will you show them, O daughter, all of the good that you do?

Will you stand up for them, when they are weary from a hard day's work?

O daughter of courage, will you stand up for them, when their faces are covered with dirt?

DAUGHTER OF COURAGE

O daughter of courage, will you stand up for My people, when they are threatened?

Will you stand up for My children, when evil doers seek to harm them?

Will you stand up for Me, when they disrespect My name?

Will you stand up, My daughter of courage, when My little ones are being abused.

Will you stand up, when they abandon Me?

Will you lead them from sin, so that I can set them free?

Will you offer them food, when times are hard?

Will you tell them, that I will protect them, like a devoted guard?

DAUGHTER OF COURAGE

O daughter of Mine, I Will give you courage, in times of need.

So that you can deliver My holy seed.

My words are the seed that I want you to plant,

So that all of My children, will sing a holy chant.

I want all of My daughters to live a holy life, so that they can conquer disputes in times of strife.

Deliver My seed to every nation.

So that I can abide in My children, from generation to generation.

DAUGHTER OF COURAGE

Climb aboard My ship of love, O daughter of courage, so that I may

show you the many places where My love is forgotten.

O daughter of courage, I will take you to the remote places of the

world, where My lost sheep are searching for Me.

I will tell you My messages of peace and hope, so that you can

deliver them to My sons and daughters of every nation.

O daughter of courage, do not be afraid of their foreign words,

because I will help you understand them.

Do not be afraid to travel with your Lord, O daughter of great

courage.

CHAPTER TWO: DAUGHTER OF JUSTICE

O little daughter of Mine, are you afraid to cry out for justice?

Are you afraid to express courage in their midst?

Do you run from justice, when you are put on the line?

Will you carry Jesus cross, when no one else is around?

Will you walk with the Lord, until justice abound.

Will you walk with the Lord, on the road to salvation?

Will you share His cross with every nation?

Do not be afraid to live like the Lord

so that you and His saints will be on one accord.

O daughter of justice, will you fight for Me?

So that My holy spirit will remain in thee.

DAUGHTER OF JUSTICE

O daughter of justice, will you hesitate when you are placed in a

position to speak out?

If you do, God will give you an encouraging shout.

Do not be afraid to go where you've never gone before,.

because God is the justice that's behind every door.

Do not be afraid to walk with your foes,

because God's eternal love will overcome all woes.

O sweet daughter of justice, please answer My plea.

So that My great light will permeate thee.

DAUGHTER OF JUSTICE

When justice calls, will you answer?

When hope is lost, will you search for it?

When pain is near, will you soothe it?

When darkness befalls you, will you run to My light?

When fear arises, will you conquer it?

When you are anxious, will your knowledge of Me

calm you?

When you are betrayed, or forsaken, will you call out to Me?

O daughter of Mine, will you answer the call of justice?

DAUGHTER OF JUSTICE

O daughter of the highest king, can you hear the call of justice?

Listen to her sweet call, My daughter.

Cling to her mighty word that echoes hope.

Listen to her call out to the eternal source of justice.

Listen to her cries as she calls out to her everlasting source of

hope.

Come, My sweet daughter of justice, and unite with My precious

children so that you can attend to the call of justice.

DAUGHTER OF JUSTICE

O burdened daughter of justice, look at My little ones

of all nations.

Help them, My darling daughter. Show them the Father, and

His perfect son, Jesus.

Help them, O daughter of the most high.

Tell them our secrets that will lead them to eternal happiness.

O daughter of Mine, unite with My little lost children and lead

them back to Me.

With your gift of love O daughter, offer My children the

Knowledge of perpetual hope and trust.

DAUGHTER OF JUSTICE

O sweet justice I hear your cries.

I hear your voice during the night.

I hear your voice as I search the heavens, for the eternal light.

O sweet justice, I hear you throughout the day.

I hear you, O justice, every night when I pray.

I will deliver the Lord's messages, so that you will cry no more.

I am the daughter of justice, and the hope for the poor.

DAUGHTER OF JUSTICE

Justice is crying out to you. Can you hear her, My daughter?

In the streets of despair, she cries out to you.

Can you hear the voice of justice, as you begin a new day?

Listen to her voice, O faithful daughter of Mine.

Listen, as she whispers the words, that will set My children free.

DAUGHTER OF JUSTICE

Can You hear them mock me, my God?

Can You hear them laugh at me, My Lord?

Can You hear them persecute and slander my good name, O Lord?

Father, can You hear them beat me with their words of torment, as

I deliver Your sweet messages of truth?

O great and worthy Lord, can You hear them snare at me, when I

triumph over sin?

Almighty Lord, can You hear the prayers of Your daughter of

justice as I kneel in Your holy presence?

Will You honor my requests for justice, my Love?

DAUGHTER OF JUSTICE

Father, hear the cry of Your daughter of justice.

Send forth Your sweet shield of love, my Lord.

Protect me from those who place fear in my heart.

Stretch out Your protecting hands while I'm in the

midst of their frightening company.

Shower me with Your drops of pure love, my Father, and

protect me as I walk in the company of my enemies.

Shelter me with Your sweet words of justice, O Lord, as

I approach my adversaries with fear.

DAUGHTER OF JUSTICE

O daughter of great justice, rejoice. All you, who search for

Justice, rejoice in My holy presence.

Cry out to Your Lord with hope, and He will shower the poor

with His gift of justice.

As you walk this earth of pain My daughter, cry out to your

Lord, for justice sake.

As you search the streets of the poor in spirit, cry out to your Lord,

for justice sake.

Rejoice, O daughter of justice, because your almighty King, hear

your cries for justice.

CHAPTER THREE: DAUGHTER OF LOVE

O daughter of love, do not change your loving ways because

of the way they treat you.

Continue expressing your love for all, no matter how they treat

you.

Remain faithful to your calling, O daughter of love, so that all may

know that you are truly Mine.

I will walk with you on your earthly journey so that you will

remain loving and kind to all.

I will take your hand and lead you in paradise way, because of

your sincere love for all.

O daughter of great love, I will always be with you.

DAUGHTER OF LOVE

Come, My precious daughter, and share the gift of everlasting life

and happiness with My angels and saints.

O daughter of love, run through the heavenly meadows that I

created for you.

Run with My precious and devoted saints.

Run with My trust worthy angels.

Take your seat at My heavenly table of love, and dine with

your savior and Lord.

O daughter of love, won't you share My heavenly food with Me.

DAUGHTER OF LOVE

O daughter of love and kindness, come share your gift of love

with your brothers and sisters.

Show them how to express the unconditional love that you possess.

Tell them that our Father wants all of His children to live in perfect

harmony with His love.

Tell them, O daughter of love that our Father waits patiently for

their return.

Ask your brothers to turn from their sinful ways, My daughter.

Ask your sisters to leave behind their former ways of conduct.

Tell them, My daughter, that our Father is a God of unconditional

Love.

DAUGHTER OF LOVE

Look, all you people, can you see the sincerity of My daughter's

love?

Can you imitate her loyalty to our heavenly savior?

Can you walk the walk that My faithful daughter walks?

Can you talk the talk that My devoted daughter talks?

Can you sing hymns of praise with gladness, like My daughter of

Eternal love?

Can you kneel in My holy presence, and express a sign of love

like my daughter of love?

DAUGHTER OF LOVE

O daughter of love, you are like a precious pearl to Me.

I love the way you bow down and kneel in My holy presence.

O daughter of Mine, you are the joy and delight of your

savior's heart.

O daughter of love, I long to show you off to My heavenly Angels.

We will rejoice because of your faithfulness to your eternal Lord.

O daughter of Mine, you are the light of My eyes.

DAUGHTER OF LOVE

Look up to Me, O daughter of love, as you close your precious

eyes.

Think of Me as you drift off into a peaceful sleep.

Know that I am with you during your periods of perplexity,

My darling daughter.

Know, O daughter of love, that your sufferings are temporary,

And My love is everlasting

O daughter of love, lay your sweet head on My eternal heart,

and sleep the sleep that echoes our uninterrupted union.

DAUGHTER OF LOVE

O My sweet daughter of the night, Shine your light of love that

comes from your heavenly creator.

Shine your light on your hurting brothers.

Shine your light on your suffering sisters.

O daughter of love, shine your continuous light on all of My lost

sheep.

Let all of them see your light of love, that your Father blessed you

with.

Show them how your light of love out shines the brightest star.

Let them witness the unity of our love in your light, My daughter.

DAUGHTER OF LOVE

O sweet daughter of Mine, I know the pain that you have

experienced because of your love for Me.

I know of the hurt that you have experienced because of your

commitment to your Lord.

O My precious daughter, I know of, and have caught every tear

that you have shed for My sake.

I know of your undying love that you constantly express in My

Holy temple.

O daughter of Mine, I know of your love.

DAUGHTER OF LOVE

Clap your hands O daughter of love as you approach your long

waited for home.

Come and share the gift of everlasting life with your heavenly

Father, and our Lord Jesus.

Come, and live with us in our unending light of love.

O little daughter of Mine, come and see the glory that I have

prepared for you before the foundation of the world.

O My wonderful and delightful daughter, come and see all of

My goodness.

DAUGHTER OF LOVE

I know your weaknesses My daughter. I know of your undying

love for all of My creation.

O daughter of love, let us go together and greet each one of My

wandering sheep as they search desperately for their salvation.

Let us show them the way to My Father's eternal realm of love and

joy.

Come with Me, O daughter of love, and help Me guide My lost

sheep back to our Father's safe and loving paradise.

CHAPTER FOUR: DAUGHTER OF COMPASSION

Look up to Me My daughter, when trying times approach you,
so that you can express your gift of compassion.

Hold My holy hands, as you walk down the road of despair and
pain. I want You to show your gift of compassion in the
presence of the hypocrites and evil doers.

O daughter of compassion, let your light shine at all times so
that all may witness your gift.

Exhibit your gift that I blessed you with in the company
of all men, so that they will know the beauty of our
compassion.

Share your gift of compassion with your sisters who are lost in
a world of sin.

Tell them that the Lord, will always take them in.

DAUGHTER OF COMPASSION

My daughter, when all abandon you because of your stance,

continue in your gift of compassion.

When they accuse you falsely, My daughter, I want you to

continue expressing your gift of compassion.

When they torment and persecute you, My daughter, I want you

to continue expressing your gift of compassion.

When they speak against My words of justice, I want you to

continue in your gift of compassion.

O daughter of great compassion, I want you to share your

wonderful gift with all of My children.

DAUGHTER OF COMPASSION

Do not faint or falter, My daughter, because your stance will bring

about a joyous outcome.

Your perseverance O daughter of compassion, will bring about

love, peace, and understanding of Me, says the Lord.

Do not retract your words of truth when you deliver My messages

of justice, O daughter of Mine.

Do not waver in the presence of the wicked ones, My daughter.

Grip My words with a firm understanding, because My words

will strengthen you in their presence, O daughter of great

compassion.

DAUGHTER OF COMPASSION

My daughter, do not fight back with words of hate as the

wicked ones do.

Your words of love will conquer their words of hate, says the

Lord.

Your words of compassion, will ease the painful hearts of the

wicked ones, My daughter.

Your words of compassion, will change the hearts of the

scornful ones.

Your words of compassion, will comfort the souls of the

tormenting ones.

O daughter of compassion, your words of forgiveness, will

calm the souls of the evil doers in the presence of our Lord.

DAUGHTER OF COMPASSION

O daughter of compassion, can you share with your needy

brothers your gift of compassion, so that they to can offer it

to those in need?

Can you shower your foes with your divine compassion, that's

stored in your loving heart?.

Can you show them the great blessings that you receive,

when ever you express true compassion to your enemies?

O daughter of Mine, will you offer your gift of compassion,

to My hurting daughters, as they walk the streets looking for love?

DAUGHTER OF COMPASSION

Come to Me, My daughter of compassion, when their words hurt
and oppress you.

Come to Me, My child, when they reject you because of your faith.

Come to Me, when they do not understand your servitude to all of
My children.

Come to Me, My daughter of compassion, when you hear evil
reports about your good works.

Come To Me, My love, when you become over whelmed by their
insults.

O daughter of compassion, come unto your Lord.

DAUGHTER OF COMPASSION

O daughter of Mine, I thank you for sharing your compassion with

My straying sheep.

I thank you My daughter, for offering a sacrifice for My heart

broken sheep.

I bless you My lamb, because you forgave those who persecuted

and tormented you.

O daughter of compassion, I will tell My Father of your faithfulness

to your brothers and sisters.

I will comfort you, My daughter, when you weep for My lost sheep,

says the Lord

DAUGHTER OF COMPASSION

I hear your cries of joy, My daughter, when you feel My presence
during your trials.

I hear your shouts of gladness, when you know that I am near.

I hear your songs of praise, as you express your appreciation for My
everlasting gift of compassion.

I hear the sound of your precious feet, as you dance to the beat of
My Holy music.

O My sweet daughter of compassion, I hear the beat of your
comforted heart.

O Father of compassion, Do You see Your compassionate daughter?

I will offer a sacrifice of fast for those who ridicule my love for
You, my Lord.

DAUGHTER OF COMPASSION

O daughter of Mine, Jesus is the epitome of love and compassion.

Exhibit your gift of compassion in His holy presence.

Follow His compassionate heart, as you face your foes each day.

With His gift of compassion, I will change the hearts of your

persecutors.

I will shower their hearts with the words of Jesus, as I deliver His

divine message of compassion.

I will comfort my false accusers with the love of Christ, as I share

His gift of compassion with them.

I will offer a sacrifice of fast, for those who question the

integrity of my faith.

I will offer a sacrifice of fasting for those who mock me daily.

Barbara Ann Mary Mack

DAUGHTER OF COMPASSION

O daughter of Mine, Where is your compassion when your brothers
are suffering from the sin of pride?

Will you comfort them My daughter, or will you hide?

Where is your compassion, when the evil doers are crying out for
help?

Will you rescue them, My daughter, or will you let them die on
your steps?

Where is your compassion, when they seek to destroy the daughters
of God?

Will you abandon them, My daughter, or will you shower them
with love?

CHAPTER FIVE: DAUGHTER OF MERCY

O daughter of mercy, I love the way you show your love for

your Heavenly Father.

I know the sincerity of the mercy that you offer your brothers

and sisters of all nations.

I know of your continuous merciful acts of charity, that you

offer daily.

I hear the sweet sounds of your cries of joy, as you minister to

My people.

Hold your head up high, My beautiful daughter of all nations,

and tell them of God's unending acts of mercy.

DAUGHTER OF MERCY

O beautiful daughter of mercy, tell all of My wonderful deeds,

and loving kindness.

O sweet daughter of the ever flowing river of mercy, share with

your sisters of every nation, the mercy that comes from our eternal

Savior.

O precious daughters of the eternal King, follow Me, as I ascend to

My Father's throne of continuous love and mercy.

Travel with Me over His rivers of perpetual love, so that we can

deliver His messages of mercy to His children from far away

lands.

DAUGHTER OF MERCY

Father, I will deliver Your messages of mercy, to those who have

exalted themselves above Your sheep.

I will deliver Your messages of mercy, to Your pride filled

children.

I will deliver Your messages of mercy, to Your sons of hate.

I will deliver Your messages of mercy, to those who steal from the

poor.

I will deliver Your messages of mercy, to those who distort Your

words of truth.

Father, help Your daughter, deliver Your messages of mercy to

those who are vain.

Father, help Your daughter of mercy.

DAUGHTER OF MERCY

Father, what should I do, when Your children exalt themselves

above Your mercy?

What should I do, when they exalt themselves above Your

messenger?

What should I do, when they exalt themselves above Your sons of

poverty?

What should I do, when they exalt themselves above Your

daughters on the streets?

What should I do, when they exalt themselves above Your

children of despair?

Father, what should I do, when they exalt themselves above You

and Your creation?

Father, what should Your daughter of mercy do?

DAUGHTER OF MERCY

The self exalted and pride filled men, will humble themselves

before Me, because of your mercy, My daughter.

They will soon exalt Me alone, because of your perseverance, O

daughter of mercy.

They will come to Me, when they realize their weakness, because

of your mercy, My daughter.

They will call out to Me for mercy, because of your forgiveness, O

daughter of Mine.

Share with your brothers of pride, the gift of God's divine mercy,

My kind daughter.

DAUGHTER OF MERCY

O daughter of Mine, will you share with your brothers of hate your

gift of mercy, so that they may conform to the ways of our Savior?

O daughter of mercy, will you stand beside My lost sheep, in the

midst of their evil ways?

Will you unite with your wavering brothers, so that they may

understand the true meaning of the Father's love?

Will you show My children the sanctity of spiritual mercy, My

daughter?

Will you express the true mercy, that comes with knowing the

Father and His perfect son, Jesus?

DAUGHTER OF MERCY

O daughter of mercy, I have carefully molded you into My

desired likeness.

Through the experience of your many trials, you have become

My holy daughter.

You are precious in My sight, O daughter, because you have

expressed My gift of mercy, to all who have offended or

hurt you.

I have molded you, in the spiritual image of My perfect Son.

O daughter of mercy, your service to all, is a true sign of

love for the Father, and His Son, Jesus.

Keep your stance, and proclaim the Gospel of your Heavenly

Savior all the days of your life, My daughter.

CHAPTER SIX: DAUGHTER OF TRUST

O daughter of trust, have you not seen My saving power?

Have you not witnessed the glory that reveals My existence?

Have you not communicated with your Lord for hours?

Have you not shared your love with your lost brothers and

sisters?

Have you not rejoiced in songs of praise in My holy presence?

O daughter of Mine, did you not trust in our heavenly Father

when trials became burdensome?

O daughter of Mine, did you not place all of your cares in the

hands of your mighty, Lord, and savior?

DAUGHTER OF TRUST

O daughter of trust, do not believe everyone who professes that

he represents Me

You will know My ambassadors by their conduct.

Do not trust everyone who proclaims that he loves Me.

You will know those who truly love Me, by the way they treat their

neighbors.

O daughter of trust, do not follow everyone who says that she is a

disciple of Mine.

You will know My disciples, by the way that they conduct

themselves in My holy presence.

O daughter of Mine, do not trust everyone.

DAUGHTER OF TRUST

Learn My words, and abide in My statutes, O daughter of trust,

so that you will be able to defend your faith, by the knowledge

that you possess.

Do not stray from My divine words, as your brothers have done,

My daughter.

Trust in My words, because they offers everlasting life.

My words, reveals the true nature of My divinity and power.

Do not follow the teachings of the hypocrites, My daughter,

because they seek the approval of the world, instead of their

God.

DAUGHTER OF TRUST

Do not be overly concerned, My daughter. Trust in Me, and My holy promises.

My daughter, you know that I have never abandoned you, when you called My name.

I will always keep My word, because I am the God of truth.

Put your trust in your heavenly master, because He will never lead you astray.

Take My hand, O trusting daughter, and come with Me to the land of unending tranquility.

There, you will see all of My trusting friends.

You will dine with those who have trusted in My eternal words, until their physical death.

O trusting daughter, please follow your Lord.

DAUGHTER OF TRUST

My precious daughter, let us walk hand in hand to My promise

land.

Leave behind those things that have caused you grief.

You know that I have conquered everything that troubled

you in life.

O My loving and trusting daughter, leave behind your concerns,

and follow Me to a place of everlasting happiness.

My daughter, at the appointed time, you will reap your reward

of continuous peace in My Father's kingdom.

Just trust in Me always, and keep the faith.

DAUGHTER OF TRUST

O daughter who long to see and dwell in My Father's house,

Tell all of My children that they can always count on Me, when

times get rough.

Tell them My daughter, that I will deliver them from cruel and

inhumane conditions.

Tell them that our Father sees and hears all of the mistreatment

that comes with poverty and despair.

Tell them My daughter, to trust Me, especially during their times

of torment.

Tell them to call out to Me, and I will calm their troubled souls.

O daughter of trust, tell them that I am near.

DAUGHTER OF TRUST

Teach me your virtuous gift of patience, O Lord.

Father, I know that every good and perfect thing comes from

Your mighty existence.

Father, I love and trust Your divine words that echoes the promises

that You whispered to me years ago.

I will remain patient and humble in Your sight, O Lord.

I believe and trust in Your words of continuous trust.

Teach Your daughter of trust Your perfect ways, so that she may

continue to hope in You, O Lord.

DAUGHTER OF TRUST

O chosen daughter of trust, My precious one.

I have chosen you among women, so that you can deliver My

messages of courage and trust.

I have chosen you, My little flower, to show all nations the

Father's glory and His will.

I have chosen you My daughter, to express the Father's will

in spite of the dangerous and trying situations.

I will give you courage My daughter, so that you will trust in Me

alone.

I will help you face your accusers and those who torment you.

I have chosen you, My daughter, to reveal the Father's existence

through your acts of humility and trust.

CHAPTER SEVEN: DAUGHTER OF COMFORT

My daughter of comfort, come and abide with your God,

so that He can share with you; His everlasting love.

Take My precious hand, O woman of great pain,

so that I can shield you from this earthly strain.

Come with Me, to My eternal kingdom.

So that I can fill you with My Heavenly wisdom

O daughter of comfort, come and rest your weary head,

on My perfect shoulders of love; your heavenly bed.

DAUGHTER OF COMFORT

Will You comfort me, O Lord, when they laugh at me?

Will You comfort me, when they doubt the promises, You

whispered to me?

Will You silence them, when they shout angry words of mockery

at me?

Will You hold me, when I'm afraid?

Will You heal, when they hurt me?

Will You raise me up, when they belittle me?

Will You speak on my behalf, when they say false things about

Your daughter?

O great God of comfort, will You comfort Your daughter, when

they bruise her eternal soul?

O daughter of Mine, I will comfort you, says the Lord!

DAUGHTER OF COMFORT

Be not afraid of My grace and mercy, O daughter of Mine!

Do not worry, when harm surrounds you.

Do not worry, when your friends and loved ones abandon you.

Do not worry, when your integrity is questioned.

Do not worry, when they ridicule you, and turn your good works

into the deeds of the world.

Do not worry, My darling daughter, when they say all kinds of evil

against your creator.

Do not worry, because I hold the key that unlocks the door to

everlasting comfort.

DAUGHTER OF COMFORT

O great God of comfort, I know that You are always by my side.

I can feel Your holy presence, as I climb the stairs of pain and

suffering.

I know that You, O Lord, of comfort, will grace me, with Your

sweet realm of eternal comfort.

You, O Lord, have offered all of Your trusting daughters, the

continuous comfort that they need, to face another day of pain.

O Lord, above, Your daughters of comfort, trust You completely.

DAUGHTER OF COMFORT

Look up to Me, My daughter, because I am your comfort in times

of despair.

Look up to Me, because I am your light when dark days appear.

Look up to Me, My love, when your day is filled with confusion

and pain.

And I will shower you with spiritual rain.

Look up My daughter, and witness the glory that awaits you.

Do you see My glory, in the people who surrounds you?

O daughter of comfort, look up to the sun, so that you can see

Heaven in the battles that I've won.

CHAPTER EIGHT: DAUGHTER OF OBEDIENCE

Persevere in My words, O daughter of the most high, and you will receive your just reward.

Hold fast to your faith and your love for Me, in spite of your many trials of suffering.

Continue walking in My ways, and you will be a witness to My eternal glory.

O daughter of obedience, I know that you are weary, because of the numerous tasks that I have given you.

I want you to know that I am well pleased with your acts of obedience, and your dedication to your Lord, and Savior.

You will receive your crown of glory that I promised to My faithful servants.

O daughter of obedience, remain faithful to Me.

DAUGHTER OF OBEDIENCE

Take refuge in My words O daughter of obedience, because they

will lead you into My glorious kingdom.

Look up to Me, as we approach your destination of sweet heavenly

bliss.

Follow Me My daughter, and show your neighbors and friends,

the importance of obeying their Father's words of love.

Tell all of My children, that obedience to the Lord, is the key to

My kingdom.

Tell them O daughter, that I long to see their faces in My paradise

above.

Tell them My daughter, to obey My words.

DAUGHTER OF OBEDIENCE

O daughter of obedience, I am pleased with your continuous works

of righteousness.

You, My daughter, have demonstrated the acts of a true servant

and friend of Mine.

Come with Me, My loving daughter, and taste the goodness of

God's Heavenly food, that is given to those who have obeyed My

words.

Know, that the reward you receives, will come from the eternal

source of true love.

Clap your hands, O daughter of obedience, as you greet your

Father, and accept your crown with gladness.

DAUGHTER OF OBEDIENCE

My Father, as I walk down Your paths of purity and life,

I will remain obedient and humble in Your presence.

I will always dwell in Your realm of divine order, as I

approach Your throne of obedience.

Let me see Your heavenly servants and friends, as I walk towards

Your city of gold.

I will always be Your daughter of obedience, my Lord, because

You have been a faithful Father to me.

DAUGHTER OF OBEDIENCE

O My obedient daughter, will you carry My words of hope to My

suffering and abandoned children?

Can you tell them that their heavenly Father, will always love and

protect them?

Tell them, that I have not turned My back on them.

Tell them My daughter, that I will always answer their cries for

justice and peace.

Tell them of My faithfulness to My suffering children.

Tell all of My children, that I hear the sound of their trusting

hearts; And their voice of hope.

O daughter of obedience, will you help My children love Me?

DAUGHTER OF OBEDIENCE

Being an obedient daughter of God, is a wonderful honor.

You, My Lord, are the source of all good gifts; And I thank

You continuously, for Your divine gift of obedience.

Teach me, My Father, how to obey all of Your commands,

so that I may offer spiritual support to my brothers and sisters.

Teach Your daughter how to walk in the paths of obedience, so

that I may live according to Your perfect will.

O Father above, help Your obedient daughter become one

with You.

DAUGHTER OF OBEDIENCE

My daughter, you have expressed your acts of obedience in everything that you do.

I have created you in My divine image, My daughter, and I will continue to bless you with the gift of obedience, all the days of your life.

To be an obedient servant of the Lord, is a divine gift from above, that should be treasured like a precious stone.

DAUGHTER OF OBEDIENCE

Father, can You teach me how to be obedient to those whom You

have placed in authority over me?

Can You guide my thoughts, so that they will not stray from

obeying You?

Will You be patient with me, My Lord, as I grow in Your gift of

obedience?

Can You teach Your daughter how to share Your message of

obedience with her neighbors?

O Father of love, can You shower all of Your daughters, with Your

gift of obedience?

DAUGHTER OF OBEDIENCE

Father, can You teach my brothers and sisters how to become an

obedient servant of Your divine words?

Can You show me how to lead them to Your path of

righteousness?

Father, help me guide Your children in the way of eternal life, so

that you can bless them with Your gift of obedience.

Father, show Your daughter how to win their hearts, so that I may

lead them to Your realm of obedience, my Lord.

DAUGHTER OF OBEDIENCE

Father, as a child, You called me into a life of servitude and obedience unto You.

My Lord, as a child they persecuted me; Will you forgive them?

When I was a child, they mocked me; Will You forgive them?

When I was a child, they bore false witness against me; Will You forgive them, my Lord?

When I was a child, they tormented me daily; Will You forgive them, my God?

Father, I will ask You over and over, to forgive those who have caused me to weep and suffer, when I was a child. Because I am Your daughter of mercy.

Father, I will obey all of Your commands, because I am Your daughter of obedience.

CHAPTER NINE: DAUGHTER WHO FEARS

O daughter of the perpetual light.

Do not fear when they call you in the night.

Stand firm to your belief in My words, which are truth.

Hold fast to the promises that I whispered to you in your youth.

Do not weep My daughter who fears,

because Your loving master is always near.

Do not let fear over power your realm of peace.

Abide in your Lord, and all of your fears He will ease

O daughter of My mighty love, you do not have to fear them,

So you can rejoice My daughter, and come unto Him.

DAUGHTER WHO FEARS

Call out to your Father, My daughter, if they persecute you for

My sake.

Run to Me, My child, because My inviting arms are always

available to you.

Hide within My pillars of love, so that I may protect you from

the snares of the wicked ones.

Do not fear, My love, because I will defend you in times of need.

I will reveal My unity with you, to all of your foes.

Do not fear them, My daughter, because I am with you.

DAUGHTER WHO FEARS

O little woman, you are so precious in My sight.

I will shield you from your afflictions, as you cry out for what is

right.

Do not be afraid of the evil one, in the form of a man.

I will conquer his evils, with the might of My hand.

They cannot harm you, O daughter of the sun.

because I am with you, and you do not have to run.

Speak against their evil ways, so that they will know,

that I live within you, and your fear will not grow.

DAUGHTER WHO FEARS

Have no fear, O daughter of the night, because your Savior,

will shine His great and holy light.

He will enlighten the lost, in their times of need.

So that they will run to Him like a lamb to his feed.

His light is pure, and clearer than glass.

His promises of hope, will always surpass.

Shine on Your daughter, O Lord of eternal light,

so that she can sing, and rejoice in Your sight.

O daughter who fears, cling to your Father because He

stands near.

DAUGHTER WHO FEARS

Look up to the heavens when evening draws near.

Rejoice, as you enter God's realm of hope without fear.

Come to Me, O daughter who fears,

so that your heavenly Father, can wipe away your tears.

O daughter of hope, come take My hand, so that I can share with

You My holy plan.

My plans for unity, peace, and hope,

for all of My daughters, to help them cope.

Barbara Ann Mary Mack

DAUGHTER WHO FEARS

Where are you today, My daughter?

Are you hiding from the pain that comes with fear?

Do not be afraid, O daughter who fears, because I will never

leave you in pain.

Do not fear My daughter, remain courageous in My sight,.

and listen to My words that will deliver you from all of your

fears.

Come out from behind the walls of your home and lift your

head up high, as you walk in the presence of those who cause you

to fear.

Place your trust in the king, because He will never flee from the

things that cause you to fear.

DAUGHTER WHO FEARS

O daughter who fears, do not be afraid when trials appear.

Because God's eternal love will conquer your fear.

Do not be afraid when you fight for justice.

Because your task is to deliver My saving message

Do not be afraid, when all abandon you.

Because Christ's Holy spirit, will see you through.

Do not be afraid to reprove the mighty men.

Because God's Holy presence will protect you from them.

DAUGHTER WHO FEARS

O daughter who fears, God is always with you, no matter

what decisions you make.

So do not be afraid to speak out for justice sake.

Do not be afraid, no matter what you have heard,

because God will give you courage to deliver His word.

Do not be afraid when darkness is around.

Because God's holy presence can always be found.

Do not be afraid to fight to the end,

because the almighty Savior, is your trust worthy friend.

DAUGHTER WHO FEARS

Father, Your cross of love is very heavy.

Please help me carry it through their streets of selfishness

and hate.

Let Your children see the pain that You bear, when they offend

You and Yours.

Help Your daughter who fear them, conquer her fears, so that she

may carry Your cross with ease.

Guide her through the narrow gates that lead to Your glory, O

Lord.

O great God of love, increase Your daughter's faith, so that she

may carry Your cross of love with joy.

DAUGHTER WHO FEARS

My Lord, the road that leads to Your sanctuary, is a road that's covered with great suffering and anguish.

I beg You, my divine love, to ease the anguish that comes with the revelations of You.

Strengthen Your daughter who fears, as she approach Your throne of holiness and glory.

Father, increase my faith, and strengthen my weak knees, as I battle for the souls of Your lost sheep.

Help me become victorious, over the evils that are present in our world today.

Father, help Your daughter who fears!

CHAPTER TEN: DAUGHTER OF HOPE

O daughter of Mine, share with your spiritual family, the gifts that I have blessed you with.

You must share with them your gifts of love, peace, and hope.

Share with them, your knowledge of My saving power, that comes with hope.

Share with them the promises that I revealed to you, pertaining to hope.

Share My sweet words, that express the true meaning of hope, in the Lord.

O My daughter of hope, enlighten My children so that they may hope in Me, as you do.

DAUGHTER OF HOPE

O daughter of hope, I hear the sound of your racing heart.

Know this, My daughter, that your God will never part.

No matter where you go, or what you do.

I will stand beside you, like a friend who is true.

Run, My daughter, into your master's arms,

so that I may comfort you, with a heart that is warm.

Take My garment, and hold on tight.

And I will send forth My love, during the night.

O daughter of hope, cling to My love.

DAUGHTER OF HOPE

Hope, is a gift that's sent from above.

Hope is the way, that the Father expresses His love.

Rejoice in hope, O daughter of the highest king.

So that you can share in His glory; And His everlasting reign.

Sing a song of gladness, as you witness God's glory.

Sing, O hopeful daughter, and tell of His holy story.

Tell of His mighty deeds, when despair is all around.

Tell of His saving power, when weakness abound.

O daughter of hope, share the glory of the Lord.

DAUGHTER OF HOPE

I hear the sounds of joy, that comes from My rejoicing daughters

I hear the sweet music that echoes the happiness that comes from

a faithful daughter.

I hear the laughter that flows from the mouths of My believing

daughters.

I hear the shouts of praise that comes from the voices of My

victorious daughters of hope.

O daughters of the eternal Word, I hear the sweet sounds of My

loving friends. Alleluia.

DAUGHTER OF HOPE

Do not be anxious O daughter of hope; Because I am the God of
continuous tranquility.

I will show you My realm of true peace and happiness.

that I promised to those who remained in My word.

Take My eternal hand and follow Me into My sanctuary of
unending bliss.

O daughter of hope, look up to Me, with the compassion and love,

that I shower you with each day.

Abide in Me, My daughter, and continue in My hope.

DAUGHTER OF HOPE

O great sender, and Father of hope. Send forth Your rays of hope,

as I enter Your holy house of prayer.

Please grace Your daughter and her brothers with Your endless

fountain of hope.

Show us Your marvelous waterfall of hope; And its ever flowing

beauty.

Father, will You meet Your children of despair on the road of

sweet hope, and greet them with Your perfect gifts of hope and

peace?

O perfect Father of hope, please greet Your children.

DAUGHTER OF HOPE

Look up to your salvation, O children of despair, and unite

with My daughter of hope.

Can't you see His holy presence in the sky?

Can't you feel His existence in your midst, O children of great

hope?

Call out to your salvation in times of despair, so that He can lift

you up.

O children of the most high, will you walk in His holy presence,

with the hope of seeing His glorious face?

Will you wait on His promises of hope, instead of fleeing?

Can you stand in His presence, with the hope of obtaining His

promises of salvation and everlasting love?

O children of hope, please come unto Me!

DAUGHTER OF HOPE

Take My hand, O children of hope, and walk with your sister,

to our God's mighty throne of hope.

Because where there is hope, there is peace.

Where there is hope, there is life.

Where there is hope, there is joy.

Where there is hope, there is love.

Where there is hope, there are rewards.

Where there is hope, there is always a spiritual gain.

Where there is hope, My daughter, there, you'll find Me.

DAUGHTER OF HOPE

Call on Me, O servant of Mine, when your in despair, and
great pain, and I will alleviate your suffering.

Where there is hope, I am in the midst.

I promised you that I would never leave you.

I am committed to you, O daughter of great hope, because
I love you.

Believe in Me, O servant of Mine, and I will give you, My
everlasting cup of hope.

Remember, O daughter, that I am with you; especially when
your thoughts are governed by despair.

Just trust in Me, O servant of hope, because I am always near.

DAUGHTER OF HOPE

When you are crying My daughter, I will always hear.

I will wipe away your fountain of tears.

I am your Lord Jesus, who comforts you every day.

Because you are My hopeful daughter, I will lead you

in salvation's way.

Come to your Lord, with a meek, and humble heart.

So that I can remove your burdens, before a new day start.

Lift up your eyes, O daughter of Mine,

so that I can heal you, by giving you a peaceful mind.

DAUGHTER OF HOPE

O perfect, and mighty God of perpetual hope.

I come to You, in Your holy presence, with the hope of

feeling Your perfect power.

I come to You with an undying faith, and a trusting heart.

I will share with Your little children the secrets of eternal

hope and joy.

O loving source of hope, I long to rejoice with my Christian

family, so that we can proclaim Your goodness throughout

eternity.

O Father of hope, will You rejoice with me?

About the Author

Barbara, has written several books within the past three months.

She attributes her compositions to the inspiration of almighty God.

Barbara believes that she was inspired to write these books, with the hope that the messages written, will permeate the Christian faith, throughout the world;

And bring back the unity that diminished over a period of time.

Barbara is a member of the Catholic faith. She was confirmed in 1999, at Saint Barnabas Church, located in Southwest Philadelphia. She is a lector at Saint Barnabas Parish; And. a contributor to several charities.

Barbara's goal is to unite all Christians, spiritually, so that they may worship almighty God on one accord.

www.ingramcontent.com/pod-product-compliance
Lightning Source LLC
Chambersburg PA
CBHW030355290526
45785CB00004B/1755